A Brief History of The United Methodist Church

*The Historical Statement From
The Book of Discipline
Approved by the 1996 General Conference*

With Introduction by Alan K. Waltz

DISCIPLESHIP RESOURCES

P.O. BOX 840 • NASHVILLE, TENNESSEE 37202-0840

www.discipleshipresources.org

Reprinted 1999
ISBN 0-88177-256-9

DR256

Contents

Introduction

This booklet contains the text of the "Historical Statement" as it appears in the 1996 edition of *The Book of Discipline of The United Methodist Church*. It provides a succinct summary of the beginning and the development of The United Methodist Church.

The "Historical Statement" first appeared in the 1968 edition of *The Book of Discipline*. It was prepared as a part of the Plan of Union that served as the basis for the 1968 merger of The Methodist Church and The Evangelical United Brethren Church. A "Historical Statement" has been included in every edition of *The Book of Discipline* since 1968. The last major revision of the "Historical Statement" was approved in 1992.

The "Historical Statement" does not attempt to be a comprehensive history of the denomination. It is designed to provide an essential outline of the key elements in the history of the people called United Methodists. It seeks to introduce the United Methodist reader to major themes and crucial events that have shaped our denomination.

In reading this brief statement, it is hoped that you will be encouraged to read further about the history and development of The United Methodist Church. Other major portions of *The Book of Discipline* include statements on doctrinal standards, theological heritage, social principles and issues, and the nature of the ministry of all Christians, including the unique roles of laity and of the ministers. *The Book of Discipline* also speaks to the organizational life of the denomination and how Christian ministry is to be carried out in local churches, in annual conferences, and at the national and world levels.

A brief list of resources is included at the end of this booklet (page 38) for those who wish to explore in greater depth the history of The United Methodist Church.

Historical Statement: The United Methodist Church

(From *The Book of Discipline of The United Methodist Church*, *1996*, pages 9-20)

On April 23, 1968, The United Methodist Church was created when Bishop Reuben H. Mueller, representing The Evangelical United Brethren Church, and Bishop Lloyd C. Wicke of The Methodist Church joined hands at the constituting General Conference in Dallas, Texas. With the words, "Lord of the Church, we are united in Thee, in Thy Church and now in The United Methodist Church," the new denomination was given birth by two churches that had distinguished histories and influential ministries in various parts of the world.

Theological traditions steeped in the Protestant Reformation and Wesleyanism, similar ecclesiastical structures, and relationships that dated back almost two hundred years facilitated the union. In the Evangelical United Brethren heritage,

1

for example, Philip William Otterbein, the principal founder of the United Brethren in Christ, assisted in the ordination of Francis Asbury to the superintendency of American Methodist work. Jacob Albright, through whose religious experience and leadership the Evangelical Association was begun, was nurtured in a Methodist class meeting following his conversion.

Roots
1736-1816

The United Methodist Church shares
a common history and heritage with
other Methodist and Wesleyan bodies.
The lives and ministries of John Wesley
(1703–1791) and of his brother, Charles
(1707–1788), mark the origin of their
common roots. Both John and Charles
were Church of England missionaries to
the colony of Georgia, arriving in March,
1736. It was their only occasion to visit
America. Their mission was far from an
unqualified success, and both returned to
England disillusioned and discouraged,
Charles in December, 1736, and John
in February, 1738. Both of the Wesley
brothers had transforming religious
experiences in May, 1738. In the years
following, the Wesleys succeeded in leading a lively renewal movement in the
Church of England. As the Methodist

movement grew, it became apparent that their ministry would spread to the American colonies as some Methodists made the exhausting and hazardous Atlantic voyage to the New World.

Organized Methodism in America began as a lay movement. Among its earliest leaders were Robert Strawbridge, an immigrant farmer who organized work about 1760 in Maryland and Virginia, Philip Embury and his cousin, Barbara Heck, who began work in New York in 1766, and Captain Thomas Webb, whose labors were instrumental in Methodist beginnings in Philadelphia in 1767.

To strengthen the Methodist work in the colonies, John Wesley sent two of his lay preachers, Richard Boardman and Joseph Pilmore, to America in 1769. Two years later Richard Wright and Francis Asbury were also dispatched by Wesley to undergird the growing American Methodist societies. Francis Asbury became the most important figure in early American Methodism. His energetic devotion to the principles of Wesleyan theology, ministry, and organization shaped Methodism in America in a way unmatched by any other individual. In addition to the preachers sent by Wesley, some Methodists in the colonies also answered the call to become lay preachers in the movement.

The first conference of Methodist preachers in the colonies was held in Philadelphia in 1773. The ten who attended took several important actions. They pledged allegiance to Wesley's leadership and agreed that they would not administer the sacraments because they were laypersons. Their people were to receive the sacraments of baptism and the Lord's Supper at the local Anglican parish church. They emphasized strong discipline among the societies and preachers. A system of regular conferences of the preachers was inaugurated similar to those Wesley had instituted in England to conduct the business of the Methodist movement.

The American Revolution had a profound impact on Methodism. John Wesley's Toryism and his writings against the revolutionary cause did not enhance the image of Methodism among many who supported independence. Furthermore, a number of Methodist preachers refused to bear arms to aid the patriots.

When independence from England had been won, Wesley recognized that changes were necessary in American Methodism. He sent Thomas Coke to America to superintend the work with Asbury. Coke brought with him a prayer book titled *The Sunday Service of the Methodists in North America*, prepared by Wesley and incorporating his revision of the Church of England's Thirty-Nine Articles of Religion. Two other preachers, Richard Whatcoat and Thomas Vasey, whom Wesley had ordained, accompanied Coke. Wesley's ordinations set a precedent that ultimately permitted Methodists in America to become an independent church.

In December, 1784, the famous Christmas Conference of preachers was held in Baltimore at Lovely Lane Chapel to chart the future course of the movement in America. Most of the American preachers attended, probably including two African Americans, Harry Hosier and Richard Allen. It was at this gathering that the movement became organized as The Methodist Episcopal Church in America.

In the years following the Christmas Conference, The Methodist Episcopal Church published its first *Discipline* (1785), adopted a quadrennial General Conference, the first of which was held in 1792, drafted a Constitution in 1808, refined its structure, established a publishing house, and became an ardent proponent of revivalism and the camp meeting.

As The Methodist Episcopal Church was in its infancy, two other churches were being formed. In their earliest years they were composed almost entirely of

German-speaking people. The first was founded by Philip William Otterbein (1726–1813) and Martin Boehm (1725–1812). Otterbein, a German Reformed pastor, and Boehm, a Mennonite, preached an evangelical message and experience similar to the Methodists. In 1800 their followers formally organized the Church of the United Brethren in Christ. A second church, The Evangelical Association, was begun by Jacob Albright (1759–1808), a Lutheran farmer and tile-maker in eastern Pennsylvania who had been converted and nurtured under Methodist teaching. The Evangelical Association was officially organized in 1803. These two churches were to unite with each other in 1946 and with The Methodist Church in 1968 to form The United Methodist Church.

By the time of Asbury's death in March, 1816, Otterbein, Boehm, and Albright had also died. The churches they nurtured had survived the difficulties of early life and were beginning to expand numerically and geographically.

The Churches Grow
1817-1843

The Second Great Awakening was the dominant religious development among Protestants in America in the first half of the nineteenth century. Through revivals and camp meetings sinners were brought to an experience of conversion. Circuit riding preachers and lay pastors knit them into a connection. This style of Christian faith and discipline was very agreeable to Methodists, United Brethren, and Evangelicals who favored its emphasis on the experiential. The memberships of these churches increased dramatically during this period. The number of preachers serving them also multiplied significantly.

Lay members and preachers were expected to be seriously committed to the faith. Preachers were not only to possess a sound conversion and divine calling but were also to demonstrate the gifts and skills requisite for an effective ministry. Their work was urgent and demanding. The financial benefits were meager. But, as they often reminded one another, there was no more important work than theirs.

The deep commitment of the general membership was exhibited in their willingness to adhere to the spiritual disciplines and standards of conduct outlined by their churches. Methodists, for example, were to be strictly guided by a set of General Rules adopted at the Christmas Conference of 1784 and still printed in United Methodism's *Book of Discipline*. They were urged to avoid evil, to do good, and to use the means of grace supplied by God. Membership in the church was serious business. There was no place for those whom Wesley called the "almost Christians."

The structure of the Methodist, United Brethren, and Evangelical Association churches allowed them to function in ways to support, consolidate, and expand their ministries. General Conferences, meeting quadrennially, proved sufficient to set the main course for the church. Annual conferences under episcopal leadership provided the mechanism for admitting and ordaining clergy, appointing itinerant preachers to their churches, and supplying them with mutual support. Local churches and classes could spring up wherever a few women and men were gathered under the direction of a class leader and were visited regularly by the circuit preacher, one who had a circuit of preaching placed under his care. This system effectively served the needs of city, town, village, or frontier outpost. The churches were able to go to the people wherever they settled.

The earlier years of the nineteenth century were also marked by the spread of the Sunday school movement in America. By 1835 Sunday schools were encouraged in every place where they could be started and maintained. The Sunday school became a principal source of prospective members for the church.

The churches' interest in education was also evident in their establishment of secondary schools and colleges. By 1845 Methodists, Evangelicals, and United Brethren had also instituted courses of study for their preachers to ensure that they had a basic knowledge of the Bible, theology, and pastoral ministry.

To supply their members, preachers, and Sunday schools with Christian literature, the churches established publishing operations. The Methodist Book Concern, organized in 1789, was the first church publishing house in America. The Evangelical Association and United Brethren also authorized the formation of publishing agencies in the early nineteenth century. From the presses of their printing plants came a succession of hymnals, *Disciplines*, newspapers, magazines, Sunday school materials, and other literature to nurture their memberships.

Profits were usually designated for the support and welfare of retired and indigent preachers and their families.

The churches were also increasingly committed to missionary work. By 1841 each of them had started denominational missionary societies to develop strategies and provide funds for work in the United States and abroad. John Stewart's mission to the Wyandots marked a beginning of the important presence of Native Americans in Methodism.

The founding period was not without serious problems, especially for the Methodists. Richard Allen (1760–1831), an emancipated slave and Methodist preacher who had been mistreated because of his race, left the church and in 1816 organized The African Methodist Episcopal Church. For similar reasons, The African Methodist Episcopal Zion Church was begun in 1821. In 1830 another rupture occurred in The Methodist Episcopal Church. About 5,000 preachers and laypeople left the

denomination because it would not grant
representation to the laity or permit the
election of presiding elders (district
superintendents). The new body was
called The Methodist Protestant Church.
It remained a strong church until 1939,
when it united with The Methodist
Episcopal Church and The Methodist
Episcopal Church, South, to become
The Methodist Church.

The Slavery Question and Civil War 1844-1865

John Wesley was an ardent opponent of slavery. Many of the leaders of early American Methodism shared his hatred for this form of human bondage. As the nineteenth century progressed, it became apparent that tensions were deepening in Methodism over the slavery question. In this matter, as in so many others, Methodism reflected a national ethos because it was a church with a membership that was not limited to a region, class, or race. Contention over slavery would ultimately split Methodism into separate northern and southern churches.

The slavery issue was generally put aside by The Methodist Episcopal Church until its General Conference in 1844, when the pro-slavery and anti-slavery factions clashed. Their most serious conflict concerned one of the church's five bishops, James O. Andrew, who had acquired slaves through marriage. After acrimonious debate the General Conference voted to suspend Bishop Andrew from the exercise of his episcopal office so long as he could not, or would not, free his slaves. A few days later dissidents drafted a Plan of Separation, which permitted the annual conferences in slaveholding states to separate from The Methodist Episcopal Church in order to organize their own ecclesiastical structure. The Plan of Separation was adopted, and the groundwork was prepared for the creation of The Methodist Episcopal Church, South.

Delegates from the southern states met in Louisville, Kentucky, in May 1845, to organize their new church. Their first General Conference was held the following year in Petersburg, Virginia, where a *Discipline* and hymnbook were adopted. Bitterness between northern and southern Methodists intensified in the years leading to Abraham Lincoln's election in 1860 and then through the carnage of the Civil War. Each church claimed divine sanction for its region and prayed fervently for God's will to be accomplished in victory for its side.

The Methodist Protestants, the United Brethren, and The Evangelical Association were not totally insulated from the slavery controversy. However, they were able to avoid the passionate struggle that fractured The Methodist Episcopal Church.

Reconstruction, Prosperity, and New Issues 1866-1913

The Civil War dealt an especially harsh blow to The Methodist Episcopal Church, South. Its membership fell to two thirds its pre-war strength. Many of its churches lay in ruins or were seriously damaged. A number of its clergy had been killed or wounded in the conflict. Its educational, publishing, and missionary programs had been disrupted. Yet new vitality stirred among southern Methodists, and over the next fifty years its membership grew fourfold to more than two million.

The African American membership of The Methodist Episcopal Church, South, had declined significantly during and after the war. In 1870 its General Conference voted to transfer all of its remaining African American constituency to a new church. The Colored Methodist Episcopal Church (now called The Christian Methodist Episcopal Church) was the product of this decision.

It was during this period that Alejo Hernandez became the first ordained Hispanic preacher in Methodism, although Benigno Cardenas had preached the Methodist message in Spanish in Santa Fe, New Mexico, as early as 1853.

The Methodist Episcopal Church did not suffer as harshly as southern Methodism did during the war. By the late 1860s it was on the verge of major gains in membership and new vigor in its program. Between 1865 and 1913 its membership also registered a 400 percent increase to about four million. Methodist Protestants, United Brethren, and Evangelicals experienced similar growth. Church property values soared, and affluence reflected generally prosperous times for the churches. Sunday schools remained strong and active. Publishing houses maintained ambitious programs to furnish their memberships with literature. Higher educa-tional standards for the clergy were cultivated, and theological seminaries were founded.

Mission work, both home and overseas, was high on the agendas of the churches. Home mission programs sought to Christianize the city as well as the Native American. Missionaries established schools for former slaves and their children. Missions overseas were effective in Asia, Europe, Africa, and Latin America. Women formed missionary societies that educated, recruited, and raised funds for these endeavors. Missionaries like Isabella Thoburn, Susan Bauernfeind, and Harriett Brittan, and administrators like Bell Harris Bennett and Lucy Rider Meyer, motivated thousands of church women to support home and foreign missions.

Significant Methodist ministries among Asian Americans were instituted during this period, especially among Chinese and Japanese immigrants. A Japanese layman, Kanichi Miyama, was ordained and given full clergy rights in California in 1887.

Two critical issues that caused substantial debate in the churches during this period were lay representation and the role of women. First, should laity be given a voice in the General Conference and the annual conference? The Methodist Protestants had granted the laity representation from the time they organized in 1830. The clergy in The Methodist Episcopal Church, The Methodist Episcopal Church, South, The Evangelical Association, and the Church of the United Brethren in Christ were much slower in permitting the laity an official voice in their affairs. It was not until 1932 that the last of these churches granted laity these rights. Even more contentious was the question of women's right to ordination and eligibility for lay offices and representation in the church. The United Brethren General Conference of 1889 approved ordination for women, but The Methodist Episcopal Church and

The Methodist Episcopal Church, South, did not grant full clergy rights until well after their reunion in 1939. The Evangelical Association never ordained women. Laity rights for women were also resisted. Women were not admitted as delegates to the General Conferences of The Methodist Protestant Church until 1892, the United Brethren until 1893, The Methodist Episcopal Church until 1904, and The Methodist Episcopal Church, South, until 1922.

The period between the Civil War and World War I also was marked by other theological developments and controversies. The holiness movement, the rise of liberal theology, and the Social Gospel movement were sources of considerable theological debate. The Methodist Episcopal Church demonstrated its regard for social issues by adopting a Social Creed at its 1908 General Conference. Social problems were also a spur in the movement toward ecumenism and interchurch cooperation. Each of the denominations now included in The United Methodist Church became active in the Federal Council of Churches, the first major ecumenical venture among American Protestants. The era closed with the world on the threshold of a great and horrible war.

World War and More Change 1914-1939

In the years immediately prior to World War I, there was much sympathy in the churches for negotiation and arbitration as a visible alternative to international armed conflict. Many church members and clergy openly professed pacifism. However, when the United States officially entered the war in 1917, pacifism faded. The antecedent churches of United Methodism were not unlike other American denominations in expressing their national loyalties.

When the war ended, the churches were again free to expend their energies in other directions. One of their perennial concerns was temperance, and they were quick to recognize it among their highest priorities. They published and distributed large amounts of temperance literature. Members were asked to pledge that they would abstain from alcoholic beverages. The United Methodist Church still encourages such abstinence.

There was significant theological ferment during this period. Liberal Protestant theology, an important school of thought in the late nineteenth and early twentieth centuries, was questioned. It was attacked by a militant fundamentalism and later by neo-orthodoxy, which accused it of undermining the very essence of the Christian message. Since all three of these theological parties— liberal, fundamentalist, and neo-orthodox —were well represented in the forerunners of United Methodism, it is not surprising that heated doctrinal disputes were present in these churches.

Despite the internal theological differences that the churches experienced, they continued to cooperate with other denominations and acted to heal schisms that had taken place earlier in their own histories. For example, a division that had occurred in The Evangelical Association in 1894 was repaired in 1922, when two factions united as The Evangelical Church. A more important union, at least by statistical measurement, took place among three Methodist bodies— The Methodist Episcopal Church, The Methodist Protestant Church, and The Methodist Episcopal Church, South. Representatives of these churches began meeting in 1916 to forge a plan of union. By the 1930s their proposal included partitioning the united church into six administrative units called jurisdictions. Five of these were geographical; the sixth, the Central Jurisdiction, was racial. It included African American churches and annual conferences wherever they were geographically located in the United States. African American Methodists and some others were troubled by this prospect and opposed the plan of a racially segregated jurisdiction.

The majority of Methodist Protestants favored the union, although it meant accepting episcopal government, which they had not had since their church was organized in 1830. Following overwhelming approvals at the General Conferences and annual conferences of the three churches, they were united in April, 1939, into The Methodist Church. At the time of its formation the new church included 7.7 million members.

Movement Toward Union 1940-1967

Although Methodists, Evangelicals, and United Brethren each had published strong statements condemning war and advocating peaceful reconciliation among the nations, the strength of their positions was largely lost with American involvement in the hostilities of World War II. Nevertheless, throughout the war many church members continued to express their disdain for violence and their support for conscientious objection.

As the war ended, the churches actively worked to secure world peace and order. Many laity, pastors, bishops, and church agencies supported the establishment of a world organization to serve as a forum for the resolution of international social, economic, and political problems. In April, 1945, their labors contributed to the founding of the United Nations.

During this era, 1940–1967, there were at least three other important matters that occupied the attention of the churches that now compose United Methodism. First, they maintained their concern for ecumenicity and church union. On November 16, 1946, in Johnstown, Pennsylvania, The Evangelical Church and The United Brethren Church were united into The Evangelical United Brethren Church after twenty years of negotiation. At the time of union, the new church included about 700,000 members. The Methodist Church was also interested in closer ties with other Methodist and Wesleyan bodies. In 1951 it participated in the formation of the World Methodist Council, successor to the Ecumenical Methodist Conferences that were begun in 1881. As expressions of their wider ecumenical commitment, Methodists and the Evangelical United Brethren became active members of the World Council of Churches, founded in 1948, and the National Council of

Churches, founded in 1950. These assemblies provided a means for their members to engage in cooperative mission and other ministries. The two churches also cooperated with seven other Protestant denominations in forming the Consultation on Church Union in 1960.

Second, the churches demonstrated growing uneasiness with the problem of racism in both the nation and the church. Many Methodists were especially disturbed by the manner in which racial segregation was built into the fabric of their denominational structure. The Central Jurisdiction was a constant reminder of racial discrimination. Proposals to eliminate the Central Jurisdiction were introduced at the General Conferences from 1956 to 1966. Finally, plans to abolish the Central Jurisdiction were agreed upon with the contemplated union with the Evangelical United Brethren in 1968, although a few African American annual conferences continued for a short time thereafter.

Third, clergy rights for women were debated by the churches. The issue was especially critical in the creation of The Evangelical United Brethren Church. The Evangelical Church had never ordained women. The United Brethren had ordained them since 1889. In order to facilitate the union of these two churches, the United Brethren accepted the Evangelical practice, and women lost their right to ordination. Methodists debated the issue for several years after their unification in 1939. Full clergy rights for women were finally granted in 1956, but it took a decade more before the number of women in seminaries and pulpits began to grow significantly. When Methodists and the Evangelical United Brethren united in 1968, the right of women to full clergy status was included in the plan of union.

As this period ended, negotiations between The Methodist Church and The Evangelical United Brethren Church were proceeding toward their anticipated

union into The United Methodist
Church.

Developments and Changes Since 1968

When The United Methodist Church was created in 1968, it had approximately 11 million members, making it one of the largest Protestant churches in the world.

Since its birth, United Methodism has experienced a number of changes in its life and structure. It has become increasingly aware of itself as a world church with members and conferences in Africa, Asia, Europe, and the United States. While its membership in Europe and the United States has declined noticeably since 1968, membership in Africa and Asia has grown significantly.

An increasing number of women have been admitted to the ordained ministry, appointed to the district superintendency, elected to positions of denominational leadership, and consecrated as bishops. In 1980 Marjorie Matthews was the first woman elected to the Church's episcopacy.

The Church has endeavored to become a community in which all persons, regardless of racial or ethnic background, can participate in every level of its connectional life and ministry.

United Methodism has struggled with a number of critical issues. It has created and refined theological and mission statements. It has discussed and acted on matters of social importance such as nuclear power and world peace, human sexuality, the environment, abortion, AIDS, evangelism, and world mission.

The Church has been concerned with the faithfulness and vitality of its worship. It published a hymnal in 1989, which included a new Psalter and revised liturgies for baptism, the Lord's Supper, weddings, and funerals. Its 1992 General Conference authorized a new *Book of Worship*. A Spanish language hymnal, *Mil Voces Para Celebrar*, was published in 1996.

The United Methodist Church represents the confluence of three streams of tradition: Methodism, the Church of the United Brethren in Christ, and The Evangelical Association. With other churches that are also members of the body of Christ, it humbly and gratefully offers up its praise to God through Jesus Christ and the Holy Spirit for creating and sustaining grace. It seeks further grace as it ministers to the world.

For Additional Reading

Affirmations of United Methodists. Nashville, Tennessee, Discipleship Resources, 1998. Order no. DR255. Available from Discipleship Resources: phone (800) 685-4370, fax (770) 442-9742, online: www.discipleshipresources.org.

Behney, J. Bruce and Eller, Paul H. *The History of the Evangelical United Brethren Church.* Nashville, Tennessee: Abingdon Press, 1979.

The Book of Discipline of The United Methodist Church, Nashville Tennessee: The United Methodist Publishing House.

Carder, Kenneth L. *Living Our Beliefs.* Nashville, Tennessee: Discipleship Resources, 1996. Order no. DR169.

Available from Discipleship Resources:
phone (800) 685-4370, fax (770) 442-9742, online:
www.discipleshipresources.org.

Custer, Chester E. *The United Methodist Primer*, Revised, Nashville, Tennessee: Discipleship Resources, 1996. Order no. DR024. Available from Discipleship Resources: phone (800) 685-4370, fax (770) 442-9742, online: www.discipleshipresources.org.

Heitzenrater, Richard P. *Wesley and the People Called Methodists*. Nashville, Tennessee: Abingdon Press, 1995.

Koelher, George E. *The United Methodist Member's Handbook*, Nashville, Tennessee: Discipleship Resources, 1997. Order no. DR219. Available from Discipleship Resources: phone (800) 685-4370, fax (770) 442-9742, online: www.discipleshipresources.org.

Norwood, Frederick A. *The Story of American Methodism*, Nashville, Tennessee: Abingdon Press, 1995.

Thurston, Branson L. *The United Methodist Way*. Nashville, Tennessee: Discipleship Resources, 1998. Order no. DR215. Available from Discipleship Resources: phone (800) 685-4370, fax (770) 442-9742, online: www.discipleshipresources.org.

_____. *A Brief Introduction to The Book of Discipline*, Nashville, Tennessee: Discipleship Resources, 1998. Order no. DR243. Available from Discipleship Resources: phone (800) 685-4370, fax (770) 442-9742, online: www.discipleshipresources.org.